Dear Teresa,

So excited to be
doing your special Event!!!

You Rock!! :)

Ray

Happiness Rocks

A Powerful Blueprint to Master the Art of Lifelong Happiness

Ricky Powell
The Happiness Guy

Happiness Rocks

A Powerful Blueprint to Master the Art of Lifelong Happiness

Ricky Powell

The Happiness Guy

LifelongHappiness
.com

∞INFINITY PUBLISHING

Copyright © 2012 by Lifelong Happiness
Photos by Maureen Benoit

ISBN 978-0-7414-7286-1 Paperback
ISBN 978-0-7414-7287-8 eBook

Printed in the United States of America

Published April 2012

Warning - Disclaimer

The purpose of the book is to educate and entertain. The author or publisher does not guarantee that anyone following the techniques, suggestions, tips, ideas, or strategies will become happy or successful. The author and publisher shall have neither liability nor responsibility to anyone with respect to any loss or damage caused, or alleged to be caused, directly or indirectly by the information contained in this book.

INFINITY PUBLISHING
1094 New DeHaven Street, Suite 100
West Conshohocken, PA 19428-2713
Toll-free (877) BUY BOOK
Local Phone (610) 941-9999
Fax (610) 941-9959
Info@buybooksontheweb.com
www.buybooksontheweb.com

For

Jenna, Emma, and Jack—You Rock!

TABLE OF CONTENTS

Acknowledgments

There are so many people who helped, either directly or indirectly, make this book possible for me. I would like to express my gratitude to them now, for without them, you would not be holding this book in your hands.

First and foremost, I would like to thank my mom, Elaine, for being my number one fan. From the day I was born until the day she passed, she gave me tremendous support, encouragement, and unconditional love so that I never had to guess whether or not I was worth believing in. She was an awesome mom and a great friend. Despite a horribly dark and traumatic childhood, she went on to be the lady who always had a smile and a good word to say for everyone. Thank you, Mom. Emma and Jack lost their grandma way too early, but I'm so grateful for the time they did have with you and all the wonderful memories you provided for them. Your spirit lives on with us everyday.

I would also like to thank my dad, Al. Dad, you provided me with the consistent, carefree attitude that I am known for today. This skill continues to serve me well everyday. Despite a difficult and challenging life, both personally and professionally, if you hadn't gone on to marry mom and gotten in that near fatal car accident that fateful Memorial Day, I would never have been born and there may never have been a Happiness Guy. I hope and pray that I make it to the ripe, old age of ninety-four as you did. What the heck, maybe with today's advances in medicine, I'll try for 194! ☺

I am also fortunate to have grown up with a stepdad that I loved very much. After my parents divorced, my mom was set up by her best friend with a man named Bob Sagman.

Bob, you were such a great role model for me. You had a great sense of humor and knew so much about so many things. I'll never forget what you said to me after you began dating mom: "Ricky, I just want you to know, I'm not out to steal your mother's love; I just want to share it." Your honesty moved me, even though I was just barely a teenager. Your memory lives on with me always.

I would also like to thank my best friend, Michael. We met and performed together in high school, then went on to do the same in college. We switched from theater majors to radio/TV/film and wound up helping with each other's film projects. Michael was a true friend and one of the happiest people I have ever known. He opened the door to my first job out of college, and working with him in the professional world was a treat and an honor. His death at age twenty-three was the most devastating event I have had to endure. He was a model friend and would have given anyone the shirt off his back. Michael inspired me in so many ways, and I credit him and my mom for the revelation that we need to enjoy every moment on earth as if it may be our last.

To my sister Alanna: we had such different experiences growing up. You walked a much darker road than I had ever known about until you shared it with me after Mom passed on. Although you have had your share of depression and challenges in life, you genuinely seem happier to me today than you ever have before. I wish you continued happiness and great health and success for all your years ahead.

To Jenna, my wife of twenty years, and my children, Emma and Jack, thank you for putting up with my reading, writing and seminar attending for so many nights and weekends. I hope the knowledge and wisdom I've gained and always try to share with you will serve you all the days of your lives. I know it may be hard to tell sometimes, but you really are the most important and precious things in my life.

Doctor Phillip Biterman helped save my life by performing an emergency appendectomy on me at the Motion Picture Hospital. Doctor Biterman, words cannot express how grateful I am to you, so please allow me to simply give you my truly heartfelt, eternal thanks.

Thanks to Amy Baker for opening the door for me at NBC. After twenty years at the company, I continue to meet exceptional people there on a daily basis.

Roy Nakano is a colleague who made Toastmasters International a reality for me at NBC Universal. I had always wanted to join the organization but never had the time. Thanks to Roy, Carolyn Cousins Goldman, and Ron Oberon of District 52 for chartering Imagination at NBC Universal Toastmasters. I am currently serving my second term as club president and have even stepped up as an area governor. Toastmasters International has opened up a whole new world for me. Had it not been for Toastmasters, I would never have had the opportunity to meet so many amazing people that are helping me shape this whole new world of writing, speaking, and coaching: Maurice DiMino, Craig Duswalt, Rick Frishman, Tom Antion and Daven Michaels to name a few.

I'd also like to thank these very important authors who have inspired me. If you haven't read their work, I highly suggest you check them out.

Viktor Frankel, Randy Pausch, Jim Rohn, Brian Tracy, Dennis Waitely, Stephen Covey, Earl Nightingale, Dennis Prager, Greg Reid, Tal Ben-Shahar, Marci Shimoff and Lisa McCourt. Several of these great individuals are no longer with us in the physical world, but their significant work will educate and enlighten generations to come.

Tony Hsieh, founder and CEO of Zappos and author of *Delivering Happiness*, has been instrumental in my fascination of bringing the culture of happiness into the corporate workplace. I reached out to his team and have made it my mission to spread the happiness culture to any business that is ready to make a positive change for their employees and their bottom line.

Filmmaker, Rochelle Marmorstein, recently came back into my life. Our grandparents married over thirty years ago and that is how we first met. After they both passed, we lost touch for many years only to re-connect with each other through the work that we are both doing. Rochelle is making an important and moving film called, The Shift. You can see her awesome trailer at http://www.theshiftmovie.com. Rochelle, you have become such an inspiration to me. Thank you.

I have had the pleasure of gaining so many friends and supporters over the past few years, it would be impossible to name them all, but I would like to express my thanks and gratitude to Cindy Ashton, Mary Cimiluca, Alex Vesely, Hidi Lee, Marcia Bruce Bush, Brian Kelly, Kathy Stover, Mary Barnett, Ellen Reid, Susan Levin, Alan Skidmore, Casey Eberhardt, Carol McManus, Mary McManus, Linda P. Jones, Heather Wieshlow, Cheryl Maloney, DJ DeBellis, Shelli Weeks, Felice Cellini, Nancy Matthews, Carrie Gray-Stewart, and Robert Finkelstein. You have all helped me along this journey more than you know. I thank you for your continued support and friendship.

I would be remiss if I did not thank Mark Zuckerberg. I believe he has done more for advancing the happiness of people worldwide through the creation of Facebook than any other creation has in modern times. I have connected with so many positive, like-minded people, both personally and professionally. It has been proven that your social network can and does contribute to your overall happiness in life. May I just say that through my social network, via my personal page (facebook.com/LifelongHappiness) and my "Like" page (facebook.com/MastermindsOfLifelongHappiness), I have found more joy and inspiration from the input of others than I could ever hope to express. I hope you'll find me there soon.

If you haven't yet registered on Facebook, why not give it a try? You'll be amazed at what, and who, you can find there.

For everyone else who belongs in these acknowledgments, you know who you are. Please accept my humble gratitude for all that you have given me. I appreciate your love and support and hope that my work here will make you proud.

PART ONE

Why I Wrote This Book

Before I share the idea of *Happiness Rocks* with you, I'd like to bring you up to speed on why I wrote this book and exactly how I got here.

You should also know that by the time our work here is done, you'll know exactly why you should consider writing a book of your own. If that sounds good, I'll do whatever I can to help get you there.

In the meantime, let's get started.

A misconception that some unhappy people have is that happy people have had it easier. The truth is, this is not the case. Most of us have suffered our share of pain and loss in the world.

Life is a series of events. The secret lies in how you respond to these events. It comes down to about 10 percent of what happens and 90 percent how you respond.

My journey began on August 10, 1962, in Monterey Park, California.

My dad, Alvin Powell, worked about twelve hours a day in a broken-down, hot, and uncomfortable dry cleaning plant that he owned. I eventually learned he was unable to earn a living, despite the fact that he poured every ounce of energy into that small, unsuccessful store.

My dad had been married twice before he married my mom, Elaine. However, he could not have children due to a physiological complication.

My mom married her first husband at the age of seventeen and had two children with him, Barry and Alanna. Mom didn't stay married to their father for long because he was abusive to all of them.

She met my dad as a customer at his store, and they eventually married. Eight years later, they were on their way to a Memorial Day party when a drunk driver broadsided them and broke my dad's arm and several ribs. Less than a year later, I was born. The doctor said the accident had miraculously jarred something loose in my dad, and the rest is history. Yes, it's true: I am the result of a drunk driving accident.

When I was four years old, I pointed to the TV one day and said, "I want to be in there!" Somehow, I knew I was destined to be on television. (Little did I know that years later my true destiny would be to become a published author, speaker and professional happiness coach.)

Shortly after this epiphany, my mom's best friend moved from Monterey Park to the southeast end of Beverly Hills and suggested my mom do the same because of the great school system for which the city was known.

Luckily, my grandfather liked the idea, too, so he bought a duplex about two blocks inside the border of Beverly Hills. My grandparents moved in upstairs, and we moved in downstairs.

By this time, my very unhappy brother, Barry, who had run away several times before he was eighteen, ran away for good, and we had no idea if he was dead or alive. You can imagine what this did to my mom. Although I did crack my head open a couple of times before I was five, losing my brother was my first experience with a very unhappy event.

After I started school, the stars aligned for the second time in my life (the first time was my birth as the result of the drunk driving accident).

My first grade teacher announced one day that we were going to have a new student joining us. She asked us to treat him nicely and make him feel at home.

His name was Marc Copage, and he was on a TV series called *Julia*. We became fast friends. His dad spoke with my mom to help me get an agent.

One thing led to another, and at the age of seven, I landed a guest role on my favorite TV show at the time, *Bewitched*. After that, I went onto have a wonderful career as a child actor. I was privileged to have worked with some of the biggest stars in Hollywood: Edward G. Robinson, Henry Fonda, Fred MacMurray, Bob Hope, Michael Landon, Ron Howard, and even Tom Cruise. One of my favorite claims to fame is that I was the first kid to say, "Leggo my Eggo," in Kellogg's first Eggo Waffle commercial.

As I got older, the work started slowing down. Things became quite discouraging, and by eighteen, I was already thinking about my Plan B. Can you imagine? Eighteen is way too young to be thinking about a Plan B.

Beverly Hills High School was and still is a who's who of celebrity families. I joined the drama department immediately (what else would a Jewish, nonathletic, actor/singer/dancer/ham do?).

We performed the musical *The Music Man* in my senior year. I landed the role of Marcellus (played by Buddy Hacket in the movie). My good friend Michael was cast as Harold Hill. Michael was the son of the famous singing duo, Steve Lawrence and Eydie Gorme. After having a blast doing that show together, Michael and I attended California State University, Northridge, together. We went in as theater majors, performed in one musical on campus, and then we transferred to the radio/TV/film department to focus more on writing, production, and post-production.

We became the best of friends at CSUN. In fact, Michael was like the brother I never had. He was the most fun, compassionate, and selfless person I had known.

After graduation, Michael got a job at a well-known production company, which was co-owned by a friend of his family. Six weeks later, I hadn't yet found a job. I was at home, in bed with a 102-degree fever and no voice. The phone rang. It was Michael. He said they needed a post-production runner and this was my big chance to get into the company.

I told him I was sick, but he said it didn't matter. I called for an interview and went in that afternoon. The executive in charge of production looked at my résumé and said, "This is a nice résumé, but honestly, your friend Michael recommended you, so you're hired. Can you start tomorrow?"

I was so excited. I was about to start working with my best friend after spending years together in high school and college. It didn't get any better than that. Soon enough, I began delivering tapes to edit sessions and to the networks for shows such as *Benson, It's a Living*, and *The Golden Girls*.

Michael and I were having a wonderful time working together. Then one day he came into the office and said I wouldn't believe it: he and one of the producers sold an episode of *It's a Living* they had written together. I'll never forget his next words: "Ricky, do you know what this will do for our career?"

Unfortunately, this particular story, written in a book about happiness, has a sad ending. On February 5, 1986, at eight in the morning, I was at work in the post-production office when I received the worst call of my life.

"Michael Lawrence had a heart attack and died this morning."

At first, the news didn't compute. There was no way I could have heard those words.

"What?" I asked.

"Why don't you come downstairs?"

I was given the details.

Never before had so many emotions rushed through my head at once, but all I could say was, "Where are his parents?"

"They are in the middle of the country on tour and are flying home. Ricky, anything you need, we are behind you one hundred percent."

I screamed, "I have to go to his house!" I sprinted across the studio to the parking lot, jumped in my car, and sped down Sunset Boulevard from Hollywood to Beverly Hills. Throughout the entire drive, I cried at the top of my lungs: "Why him? Why not me?" I had done so many stupid things as a kid in high school and college that I should have been dead a hundred times already.

Michael never took a drug. He never smoked. He was an athlete, played every sport, was a martial artist, and yet—he was gone. It just wasn't fair.

To this day, that was the most devastating event I have lived through. Losing your best friend at any age sucks more than words can describe.

Of course, it doesn't stop there. Many other unhappy events happened along the journey to where I am today. I normally never discuss them, but since it's just you and me, I'll make a partial list. Okay, here it goes:

"The Happiness Guy's List of Less Than
Happy Life Events"

Ages 6 to 9: I was bullied in school, relentlessly
Age 13: My parents divorced
Age 13: My grandma died
Age 16: I failed my driving test…twice…on my birthday
Age 16: I was in my first car accident
Age 18: My grandfather committed suicide
Age 23: Best friend died suddenly

From here, I won't break it down by age, but suffice it to say, there have been several car crashes, multiple trips to the ER, losing both of my parents, and a painful financial disaster, which was the result of a betrayal of trust by someone who I thought had been a friend.

I also had a painfully long, nine-year ordeal with a workplace bully which, believe it or not, brought me to the place in my life where I am now known as, "The Happiness Guy."

That's a story for another time, but let me just say this: I believe there are no coincidences in life. Everything happens for a reason. Good or bad. Some things are more easily explained, while others, like losing a loved one too early, are impossible to fully comprehend.

Oh, one other thing. In 2007, I became violently ill one morning, went to the emergency room, and was sent home after being told it was just food poisoning. As it turns out, I had been walking around for two weeks with a ruptured appendix. I spent the next six days in the hospital recovering from surgery, during which the doctor removed the tiny stub of leftover appendix. I consider myself so incredibly lucky to be alive today. There are no words to describe my gratitude to God and my surgeon.

Honestly, I could go on, but I think I've made my point. Life is not always easy. Life can be tough, without a doubt. However, how you choose to react or respond to what has happened is completely up to you.

One important thing I'd like to share is that I am not saying any pain I've experienced in my life compares to or is worse than the pain you or anyone else has felt. We all carry our own set of circumstances that have led us to exactly where we are in life at this moment.

In the pages that follow, I will go over what I have learned are the best tips and techniques for living a life filled with happiness and meaning.

I believe that living each day feeling as happy as possible is more than just an important skill to possess. I believe it is truly an art to be mastered. I also believe that if you put in the work required (yes, I used that four-letter word), you will live a much richer and more profound life.

It is my fondest wish that you find Lifelong Happiness deep down in your soul and share it with the world. That's exactly what I'm doing right now. Won't you join me?

INTRODUCTION

Happiness Rocks

A Powerful Blueprint To Master
The Art of Lifelong Happiness

The Birth of *Happiness Rocks*

Once upon a time (about 384 B.C.), in a land far, far away (Stagira, Macedonia, now known as Greece), a great philosopher named Aristotle said, "Happiness is the meaning and the purpose of life, the whole aim and end of human existence."

I have always loved that quote. Honestly, though, it is a mouthful. I thought it would be nice to take the wisdom and meaning of what Aristotle said and distill it into an idea that would be simple enough for all us non-philosophers to understand and, more important, remember.

Then it came to me...Happiness Rocks! Simple enough, right? When you love something, you say, "That Rocks!" When you love someone you say, "You Rock!"

I'm hoping that once this idea catches on, "Happiness Rocks" will become a household phrase. Of course, I'll help it along in any way I can: tee shirts, mugs, and bracelets. Anything to help the cause! ;)

We'll Do Anything To Be Happy

Think about it. Everything we do, everyday of our lives, is ultimately to make ourselves feel happy. We spend years in school in order to get a good job so we can make a good living to buy the things we want to be happy. We spend years dating to find our soul mate so that we can get married, have a family, and live happily ever after. Happiness is something we all want. We want as much of it as we can get, and we want it to last forever.

We often end up achieving many of these things, yet we still end up feeling unsatisfied, unfulfilled, or frustrated—definitely *not* happy.

If you've ever spent one minute thinking that Lifelong Happiness is an elusive, mysterious, out-of-reach pipe dream, think again.

Not only is happiness readily available in any moment you choose, it can also be your springboard for creating success in every area of your life. That is precisely what you are going to learn in this book.

One common misconception many people make is that they will be happy once they are successful. The truth is, to be a true success you must find happiness first. Once you are happy, deep in your soul, success can follow in everything you do.

Sound simple? It is. Sound easy? Uh, not so fast. You see, happiness is not always a slam-dunk. However, the great news is that Lifelong Happiness can be thought of as an art form that can be mastered with skills that can be learned, practiced, perfected, and shared.

If I were to tell you happy people tend to make more money, have better relationships, stay healthier, and live longer, would that inspire you to take a deeper look into the science of happiness and study the skills involved in order to master it as an art form?

Well, I'm telling you now, it's true. I'm also thinking your answer to the above question is probably "yes," or you wouldn't have picked up this book.

Your Mission: Please Accept It!

Please do me a favor and promise yourself something right now. I'd like you to promise YOU that you will commit to the idea that this will work for you and that nothing will stand in the way of your achieving the kind of happiness you have been dreaming about. Whatever you do, please don't allow this guide to become shelf help. You know what I'm talking about. The kind of book or program you invest in, then put on a shelf in your house or apartment only to gather dust and take up space.

With patience and perseverance, along with the tools you will find in this book, you can achieve success in every area of your life simply because you've allowed happiness into your soul in a way you never have in the past.

I'm going to be completely honest with you because I know you can handle it. This may not be the easiest thing you have · ever done.

However, together we can make it fun, and I promise that if you follow through, open yourself up to the limitless possibilities that are before you, and just don't quit, you WILL win. You WILL succeed. You WILL become a role model for so many others who are looking for the answers just like you are right now.

The truth is, some of the suggestions in *Happiness Rocks* may well prove to be a tough challenge. Nonetheless, your ultimate results will astound, delight, and quite honestly make you a much greater, deeper, and more fulfilled person. Your value to yourself and the world will increase beyond measure.

The ideas contained in this book are invaluable tools for you to use on your road to happiness. They can either stand alone as your single resource for the journey you are about to undertake, or they can be used in conjunction with the complete *Happiness Rocks Home Study Course*. The entire course includes the printed book you are reading now, a downloadable ebook version, a set of CDs that contains all of the information in an easy-to-use, on-the-go audio format, a comprehensive thirty-day action guide, and one ticket to my live seminar where I will be delivering the ideas from *Happiness Rocks* on stage in an interactive, fun, and engaging format. If you are unable to attend in person, you'll have access to a recording of the live event online, accessible whenever you wish.

You may also want to consider taking a spot in my upcoming Happiness Rocks Master Mind group or even becoming a client of my one-on-one Happiness Rocks Coaching Program.

I hope you will take advantage of everything this course has to offer. Making an investment like this in yourself will bring infinite returns.

Finally, I'd like to say, "Thank You" and "Congratulations." Thank You for believing in yourself and your future enough for you to have opened this book and read this far. Congratulations for embarking on a journey that will transcend everything you have ever learned, thought, or settled for regarding happiness and success.

Now, if you're ready, it's time to learn the powerful blueprint to master the art of Lifelong Happiness. Sound good? Great, let's get started!

PART TWO

The Happiness Rocks Blueprint

H - Happiness Habits Worth Having

"Happiness is a habit—cultivate it."

~ Elbert Hubbard

What is a habit, exactly? The dictionary defines it as, "An acquired behavior pattern regularly followed until it has become almost involuntary." Like it or not, we all have them. Normally, what comes to mind when someone mentions the word "habit" is something negative. However, there are countless awesome habits that would be well worth your time to have. We'll explore many of these in this chapter.

Take Good Care

The first happiness habit worth having is probably the most important. You've got to take good care of yourself. There are so many elements that go into creating and sustaining great mental and physical health. Good health is instrumental when it comes to happiness. Here are some of the crucial, yet often ignored factors (and their benefits) you should consider when striving for a healthy and happy life.

Proper Nutrition
  ~ Helps you maintain a healthy weight
  ~ Provides energy
  ~ Promotes good sleep

Dietary Supplements
  ~ Help you overcome nutritional deficiencies
  ~ Help boost your immune system
  ~ Help eliminate toxins from your body

Daily Exercise
  ~ Increases self esteem
  ~ Increases mental focus
  ~ Decreases stress levels

Ricky Powell, The Happiness Guy

Meditation
- ~ Lowers oxygen consumption
- ~ Decreases respiratory rate
- ~ Increases blood flow and slows the heart rate

Yoga
- ~ Increases flexibility and strength
- ~ Improves posture
- ~ Elevates mood

Visualization
- ~ Brings calmness to your mind
- ~ Reprograms your subconscious
- ~ Creates the life you want

Affirmations
- ~ Challenge negative beliefs
- ~ Reprogram your thought patterns
- ~ Experience positive changes in many aspects of your life

Examples:
- * I am always positive, truthful and helping others.
- * I have an amazing job that fulfills me on so many levels.
- * I am ready and willing to release the past, now.
- * Loving myself heals my life.
- * I nourish my mind, body, and soul.
- * I attract only healthy relationships.
- * My life is joyful and filled with love, fun, and friendship.

Random Acts of Kindness

When you are kind to others, the happiness returned to you is immeasurable. Making a habit of performing random acts of kindness for friends, coworkers, and especially strangers should be at the top of everyone's list of positive habits to acquire. Here are just a few items on the list:

* Donate your time
* Support a worthy cause
* Pay someone a sincere compliment
* Thank someone for his service

Use the Magic Words

When my kids were little, we used to watch *Barney the Purple Dinosaur* together. One of my favorite Barney songs was the "Please and Thank You" song. The lyrics were something like, *"Talkin' 'bout Please and Thank You, they're called the magic words, if you want nice things to happen, they're the words that should be heard,"* and it went on from there. I *always* use these words, and I highly recommend you do, too. It's so simple, yet some people forget or even find it hard to do. I have always found these words work wonders. Please and thank you will never go out of style.

Other magic words include, "I Love You," "I'm Sorry," "I Appreciate You," "How Can I Help?"

The Power of Forgiveness

Forgiveness is such an important habit to possess. Harboring anger hurts only one person: the person who is angry. Most people think that when they are mad at someone and act out on that anger, they are punishing the person at which the anger is directed. In reality, the anger tends to fester and grow inside the person holding onto it.

My feeling is that holding onto negative feelings is a breeding ground for disease. Once you can let go and forgive, you are doing yourself a tremendous favor. This doesn't necessarily mean you need to forget what happened that made you angry to begin with. It just means finding the strength to forgive so that you can get back to enjoying life.

The Golden Rule(s)

Treat others as you want to be treated. Another simple idea, yet there is a reason it's called "The Golden Rule": why would you want to treat anyone other than how you would like to be treated? Unfortunately, few people operate using this happiness habit. Please be one of them. Be polite, and if you don't have anything kind to say, don't say anything.

Expanding on the Golden Rule

Treat Everyone with Respect: Regardless of one's station in life, everyone deserves to be treated with the utmost dignity and respect. You can tell a lot about a person by the way he treats service providers. How do you measure up?

Model Great Behavior: Always behave as if you are being watched. Chances are that somewhere, somehow, you are. Were you given the wrong amount of change? Does someone need to change lanes in front of you? Are you going out of your way to do an awesome job at work? How about at home? Everywhere you go, people are watching your behavior. Make sure it's outstanding. You can't go wrong when you are modeling great behavior.

Everything Counts: Every day you are alive, you are either moving ahead or falling behind, getting closer to your goals and dreams or backsliding in the wrong direction. I implore you to think about the legacy you want to leave behind for your loved ones. How do you want to be remembered? This is an important question you must not ignore. Please take some time to think about your answer.

a - Attitude Is Everything

"Attitude is a little thing that makes a big difference."
~ Winston Churchill

The aforementioned is one of my favorite quotes from Sir Winston Churchill. The reason I like it is because it's short, simple, and true. Your attitude in life will either make or break you. How many times have you seen someone with a chip on his or her shoulder? How do you feel about them? How do you suppose others feel about them? When you stop to think about it, no one likes a poor attitude. These are the people who tend to fail in life and never seem to get ahead. Don't be one of them. You are better than that!

Begin Each Day With an Attitude of Gratitude

An important part of my Lifelong Happiness 30-Day Challenge is to write down three things you are grateful for every day. You can either do this in our Masterminds of Happiness online community or in your private journal, but please do it. It's important to be grateful for everything you have in your life. It keeps your focus positive.

Every day you wake up feeling healthy is another day to be grateful. Start appreciating the little things in life. So often it's the little things that are really the big things. The air you breathe, the water you drink, the food you eat, your friends, family, work, neighborhood, the flowers, trees, birds, heck, even bees! After all, they make honey, right?

Try this exercise: Imagine waking up tomorrow morning with only the things or people in your life for which you are grateful. How many would you lose due to a lack of gratitude?

Thank Someone Every Day

Here's a callback to the last chapter. Remember one of our magic words: *thank you.*

Everyday you should be thanking people: the people who serve you in restaurants, your mail carrier, your kid's teacher, the teller at your bank, the crossing guard, a police officer, fire fighter, or paramedic. It's important to recognize the people who make the world a better place.

You can even thank someone for smiling. Think about that for a minute. You're walking down the street, and a stranger smiles at you. You say, "Thank you." They ask, "For what?" You tell them, "For brightening my day!" I guarantee they will smile even more in the future.

Be a Winner

Although life can be difficult at times, project a winning attitude as much of the time as you can.

Don't be a victim or even pretend to be one. People don't want to hear about your bad day or bad month or even your bad year. Sure, they'll listen, but they may be thinking, "I need to avoid this drama; the last thing I need is for it to rub off on me."

Thinking this doesn't make them a bad or uncaring person. It's just human nature. We want and need to be around positive people. Like attracts like.

When you project the attitude of a winner, people will want to be around you more, and, suddenly, you will have friends everywhere you look.

Discover the Power of PMA (Positive Mental Attitude)

"A happy person is not a person in a certain set of circumstances, but rather a person with a certain set of attitudes." ~ Hugh Downs

You may have heard of the book, *Think and Grow Rich* by Napoleon Hill. This is one of the most well known, best selling books on personal wealth and lasting success ever written. It was first published in 1937. What you may not know is that Napoleon Hill co-wrote another book years later with W. Clement Stone called *Success Through a Positive Mental Attitude*. In the book, they discuss the overwhelming importance of developing and maintaining a positive mental attitude in life.

The book suggests following several success principles that can help you clear the cobwebs from your thinking, motivate yourself and others, enjoy more energy, and live a healthier and longer life. The list goes on and on. Does this sound familiar? It's much of the same information right here in *Happiness Rocks*. If you implement these ideas and practice them everyday, there is no reason that you should not or will not succeed in whatever area you choose.

Notice the Attitude in Others

Something I always do is let other people know that I appreciate their model attitudes. My wife and I were at a local restaurant not long ago, where our waiter sported a big smile, enthusiastic welcome, and let us know how well we would be taken care of. We had never seen a server demonstrate such a positive attitude. I instantly complimented him on his service and winning attitude, and he went on to tell us how much he loved his job and helping people. Just being around people like this helps you improve your own mood. When you experience this gift from others, make sure they know how much you appreciate them.

$\mathcal{P}$- People Power

"Individually, we are one drop. Together, we are an ocean."

~ Ryunosuke Satoro

People are the very essence of our world. We are all connected in one way or another, so it's crucial to get along with everyone. Using this skill will take you far on your road to happiness.

Expand Your Network

Networking has always been important. In today's fast-paced, competitive society, it's imperative. The good news is that, with so many social media tools at our fingertips, expanding your network has become child's play. Sites like Facebook, Twitter, LinkedIn, and others make it easy to connect with old friends as well as make new ones.

Value Your Relationships

As you build your network, you should be looking for ways to help people. The more you help others, the more they will want to help you. That's what true networking is all about. Motivational author and speaker Zig Zigler said, "You can get everything in life you want if you just help enough other people get what they want."

Of course, there are many types of relationships, personal and professional, with many subcategories within them. Regardless of the type of relationship you are building or engaging in, you need to treat the other person with respect, kindness, and consideration.

If You Want To Be Interesting, Be Interested

I learned this in Dale Carnegie's book, *How to Win Friends and Influence People.*

Most people love talking about themselves. When you engage in conversation with someone, find out as much as you can about him. Ask about his likes and dislikes, how he spends his time, what he does for a living, and especially, how you can help him. This will make you stand out as someone who is truly interested in a person, and that person will automatically be more drawn to you than someone else who doesn't care about him and just wants to speak about himself.

Leverage Your Connections

Here's a crazy idea: if you find that you need something, just ask. You will never know if you don't ask. One of the benefits of having a large network of connections is that you can reach out for help when you need it most.

Many years ago, I worked with someone who turned out to be a dangerous individual. He made up stories about me and had every intention of getting me fired for absolutely no reason at all. Over the years, I had developed a large network of happy customers, so I reached out to them for help. Overnight, they all came through, making calls and sending e-mails and letters on my behalf. In the end the other fellow was let go.

Let me repeat: leverage your connections.

$\mathcal{P}$- Plan Your Work and Work Your Plan

"The tragedy of life doesn't lie in not reaching your goal.
The tragedy lies in having no goal to reach."

~ Benjamin Mays

Have you ever thought to yourself, "What if things don't work out the way I planned? What's my Plan B?" Here are a few words of advice that I hope will serve you well.

Don't be so quick to give up on your Plan A. So often, when things don't go exactly as planned, we just throw in the towel and give up. In the words of Winston Churchill: "Never, never, never give up."

I was living my dream as an actor at the age of seven. I was blessed with the privilege to act in many TV shows, commercials, and even a couple of movies. As I aged into my mid-teens, things started slowing down. It became harder to land parts. All of a sudden, everyone was asking me about my Plan B. Once I began listening to that negative thinking, it was over. I threw in the towel and went to work on Plan B.

It was a great Plan B, mind you. I joined the Director's Guild of America, worked on award winning shows like the *The Golden Girls* and *Empty Nest*, and have spent over twenty years at NBC, meeting and working with some of the most talented people in the industry.

Still, my advice to you is not to give up on your dream. Keep it alive and plan to implement it over time without giving up.

My high school drama teacher serves as a wonderful example. He retired after teaching for over thirty years to become an actor. He ended up doing commercials and then got the role of Edward Quartermaine on the soap opera *General Hospital*. He even moved over to *Days of Our Lives* for a while and worked right down the hall from me at NBC. It was wonderful to see him at work all those years after my time with him in high school. He is a true testament to what you can accomplish in the Golden Years of life.

Slow and Steady Wins the Race

We've all heard the story of the tortoise and the hare. In the end, it's not speed that counts; it's persistence and fortitude, which will eventually lead you to victory.

Develop New Skills

In this age of information and technology, it's important to develop and be good at more than just one skill. Regardless of your chosen field, a few of the skills I believe are the most important in life are happiness (yes, it is a skill; it can even be an art), communication, and adaptability.

Learning more about happiness is most likely one of the reasons you picked up this book. That's a good thing, because happiness is an area that has literally become a science, through the field of positive psychology. There is so much to learn and practice in the area of creating a happy life. The great news is that it is completely your choice. You have the power to choose how you will live your life.

This morning, I was reminded of a quote from Stephen Covey: "To know and not to do is really not to know." This statement is filled with truth. It's not too early to ask yourself what you will do with the knowledge you are gaining from this book once you are done reading it. Will you commit to the rest of the program? Will you take the 30-Day Challenge? Will you apply what you are learning to ensure you will benefit from your newfound enlightenment?

I sincerely hope you put this information to excellent use and begin applying it immediately. Not only can you apply it in your own life, you can share this information with others and inspire them to do the same. We'll talk more about that in the next chapter.

First, let's quickly discuss the two important skills aside from happiness that will serve you well in your professional and personal life.

Good communication skills are essential in developing long-lasting success in all areas of your life. Frequent breakdowns in communication at work never cease to amaze me. This tends to happen because people don't always listen carefully, nor do they express themselves clearly. Learning and practicing these important skills can solve both of these problems. Toastmasters International is an excellent training ground to help you improve your communication.

The other skill I believe you should possess is adaptability. Your ability to adapt to any situation will be an asset in your career and at home.

Try it. You'll be pleasantly surprised once you learn how much more effective you will become once you learn the art of adaptability, communication, and, especially, Lifelong Happiness.

7

7 - Inspire Others

"Those who bring sunshine to the lives of others
cannot keep it from themselves."

~ James Matthew Barrie

Simply by helping and inspiring others we gain so much
more happiness for ourselves.

An Excellent Mantra: Learn, Practice, and Teach

Knowledge is power, but applied knowledge is supreme. Once you learn something worth knowing, don't just end it there with the knowledge. Practice what you've learned until you become good, then great, then awesome with that new knowledge.

Now that you've become an expert, guess what? It's time to share that knowledge with others by teaching it to them. By doing this, you will be helping to perpetuate the lifelong learning process in others and keep the positive, upward spiral going.

Happiness Is Contagious

There are so many things in this world you can either catch from others or spread to others. Many of these things are less than desirable. However, there is also something truly precious that you can share with an unlimited number of people for the rest of your life.

Once you truly live with happiness from the inside out, you can become a walking, talking University of Happiness and teach others how to ignite their own inner happiness so that they, too, may achieve success in every area of their lives.

Happiness is one habit worth catching.

Deliver a Good Message

Every time you open your mouth, you have the opportunity to stick your foot in it. Alternatively, you can say something that really counts. Why not always be there with a kind word, an encouraging thought, and a bright message?

You can make someone's day with a simple smile and a heartfelt, "Good Morning!"

Model Good Behavior

Everything counts. Chances are, you usually know the right thing to do. The question is, how often are you doing it? Many times, the right thing to do is the difficult thing to do, and we take the easy way out. I suggest not taking the easy way out. As often as you can, take the high road. You'll be a great example to those around you, and people will want to be like you. If more of us employ this behavior, it will create a trend that will do wonders for our world.

n - Never Give Up

"Never, Never, Never Give Up."
~ Winston Churchill

This is probably Churchill's most famous quote made during World War II, on never giving up. Ideas don't get any simpler. The only way to fail is to quit. As long as you keep trying, you cannot fail.

Winners Never Quit...

You know the rest, right? Quitters Never Win. This is a quote from Vince Lombardi, one of the greatest football coaches of all time.

Both of these quotes carry a similar message that is important when it comes to happiness and success. The message? Slow and steady wins the race.

Some Encouraging Statistics on Persistence

Colonel Sanders was driven out of business in 1967 due to the construction of a new road. He went to over a thousand places trying to sell his chicken recipe before he found a buyer interested in his eleven herbs and spices. Seven years later, at the age of seventy-five, Colonel Sanders sold his fried chicken company for a finger lickin' $15 million.

Walt Disney was fired by a newspaper editor for lack of ideas and went bankrupt several times before he built Disneyland.

Henry Ford failed and went broke five times before he finally succeeded.

Every movie studio in Hollywood rejected *Star Wars* before 20th Century Fox finally agreed to produce it. It went on to become one of the highest-grossing movies in film history.

After Fred Astaire's first screen test, a memo from the casting director of MGM, dated 1933, read, "Can't act! Slightly bald! Can dance a little!" Astaire kept that memo over the fireplace in his Beverly Hills home.

Babe Ruth, considered by sports historians to be the greatest athlete of all-time and is famous for setting a home run record, also held the record for the most strikeouts.

Eighteen publishers turned down Richard Bach's *Jonathan Livingston Seagull* before Macmillan finally published it in 1970. By 1975, it had sold more than seven million copies in the United States alone.

More than twenty-five publishers turned down Margaret Mitchell's classic, *Gone with the Wind*.

Richard Hooker worked for seven years on his humorous war novel *M*A*S*H*, only to have it rejected by twenty-one publishers before Morrow published it. It became a runaway bestseller, spawning a blockbuster movie and a highly successful TV series.

When the first *Chicken Soup for the Soul* book was completed, thirty-three publishers in New York turned it down and another ninety at the American Booksellers Association convention in Anaheim, California, before Health Communications, Inc., finally agreed to publish it. The major New York publishers said, "It is too nicey-nice" and "Nobody wants to read a book of short little stories." Since that time more than eight million copies of the original *Chicken Soup for the Soul* book have been sold. The series, which has grown to thirty-two titles, in thirty-one languages, has sold more than fifty-three million copies.

Lucille Ball was dismissed from drama school with a note reading, "Wasting her time, she's too shy to put her best foot forward."

Cut from the high school basketball team, Michael Jordan went home, locked himself in his room, and cried.

A teacher once told Thomas Edison he was too stupid to learn anything and that he should go into a field where he might succeed by virtue of his pleasant personality.

His fiancée died, he failed in business twice, he had a nervous breakdown, and he was defeated in eight elections. None of that mattered to Abraham Lincoln.

You get the message, right? DON'T QUIT!!

$\mathcal{E}$ - Excuses Be Gone

"You must take personal responsibility.
You cannot change the circumstances, the seasons,
or the wind, but you can change yourself.
That is something you have charge of."

~ Jim Rohn

Take Responsibility

When you take responsibility for your actions and your life, it is quite liberating. You need to realize that you are where you are right now in life because of the exact things you have done to this point.

Stop Blaming Others

When you point your finger at someone else, you have three fingers pointing back at yourself. Blaming others accomplishes nothing more than complicating things and destroying good will. Please don't do it.

Take Action Now

You can talk all you want, but until you take action and accomplish what you have set as your goal, nothing happens. Action is where it's at. Going through this program is a perfect example. You had enough interest to move into action, bought the book or program, and have gotten this far in reading it.

However, unless you finish the material, make a lifelong study of it, and move into action by implementing the ideas presented here, nothing will happen. If you were content with staying in your current situation, I doubt you would have invested in *Happiness Rocks*.

By following the ideas in this book, you should start seeing and feeling the results very quickly. How quickly depends completely on you. Remember: take responsibility.

S - Serve Others

"He who wishes to secure the good of others
has already secured his own."

~ Confucius

I have found that one way of generating happiness from within is to get out of your "self." When you stop focusing on yourself and what you think you may be missing and start focusing on others and begin to ask what you can do to help bring them what they truly need, you can't help but start to feel good.

You have the power to change other's lives, which is a powerful way to look at the world.

Volunteer Your Resources

You don't need a big pile of cash to help others. There are so many ways to offer support.

Time is one of the best commodities you can donate. People need your time. Whether it's helping to assemble care packages for soldiers overseas or just providing an outreached hand and friendly smile for someone at a senior center or in a hospital, you can help make someone's day so much brighter and give them the hope they may need.

Raise Awareness

Another way of helping is to spread the word about a cause that is important to you or someone you love. Today more than ever, social media is making it simple to highlight what is important to you and get that all important message out to the world.

You can truly raise awareness on a global scale. All it takes is the desire and setting your mind on the goal. Then take action and you're there.

By raising awareness, you can leverage your effort and help move the cause forward much faster than if you were working alone.

Give What You Can

Charitable causes always need money. If you are able to donate even small amounts, it will always be greatly appreciated. There are so many worthy causes in the world. Donating some of your hard-earned currency will not only make a big difference to whatever cause you are supporting, it will make you feel so much better.

Studies have shown how giving as little five dollars can elevate your mood. Try it and see what happens.

$\mathcal{S}$ - Stay Focused on What Matters

"You become what you think about."
~ Earl Nightingale

Earl Nightingale, the father of personal development, explained in his book *The Strangest Secret* how we become what we think about. For example, a farmer owns land containing rich, fertile soil and plants two crops. One is corn; the other is nightshade, a deadly poison. He waters them both and takes care of the land. Both grow and return exactly what was planted in the field.

Your mind is the same as the rich soil. You can plant positive thoughts (corn) or negative thoughts (nightshade). Your mind will return exactly what you plant. Positive thoughts of success, gratitude, and achievement or negative thoughts of worry, fear, and doubt. Your mind doesn't care what you plant, but it will return what you plant. The choice is entirely yours.

It's the Little Things

Smiling for a stranger. Hugging an old friend. Kissing your kids or your parents. Any of these actions can brighten someone's dark day. All it takes is the smallest amount of attention. It's attention to the little things that count.

Everything Counts

Speaking of counting, everything counts: holding a door open, how you treat others, how you treat yourself, random acts of kindness. Always act as if someone is watching. Chance are, someone is.

Living *The Dash*

The Dash is one of the most widely known poems. I first heard it read at my father's funeral.

It begins:

I read of a man who stood to speak at the funeral of a friend. He referred to the dates on her tombstone from the beginning to the end.

He noted that first came the date of her birth and spoke of the following date with tears, but he said what mattered most of all was the dash between those years.

Have you ever considered how you want to be remembered? What would you like your legacy to be?

It all begins with how you live your life and how you treat people. Remember: people may forget what you said; they may even forget what you did; however, they will never forget how you made them feel.

Start making your dash count a little more every day.

$\mathcal{R}$ - Reinvent Yourself

"Reinventing the wheel doesn't work.
Reinventing yourself does."

~ Ricky Powell, The Happiness Guy

Take Stock of Where You Are

Are you happy with the results you have achieved so far? Would you like more? It may be a good idea to really take a close look at what your life looks like today and evaluate whether a good personal and/or professional makeover could be right for you.

Just because you have lived a certain way until now doesn't mean you are obligated to stay that way.

The definition of insanity is doing the same thing over and over and expecting a different result.

The only way to get a different result, a better result, is to change.

You may be familiar with the famous quote that is attributed to Gandhi: "Be the change you wish to see in the world."

As I understand it, he actually said something like this: "We but mirror the world. All the tendencies present in the outer world are to be found in the world of our body. If we could change ourselves, the tendencies in the world would also change. As a man changes his own nature, so does the attitude of the world change towards him. This is the divine mystery supreme. A wonderful thing it is and the source of our happiness. We need not wait to see what others do."

If you seek change, but don't know how to get started, the *Happiness Rocks Home Study Course* is an ideal first step. Of course, I'm biased, but I'm hoping that once you learn and practice this material, you will agree. This course can be a great catalyst for change.

Sprinkle in Some Dreams

A dream is a big idea with a strategy. A fantasy is a big idea without a strategy.

Having one or more dreams to focus on is important. I suggest that you first create a dream you would love to see come true. It's the big picture. Something like, "I want to meet my soul mate and live happily together for years to come. I want to launch my own business and obtain the financial freedom I am seeking. I want to reach my ideal weight and live in excellent health for the rest of my life."

Dreams are an essential part of life. Without big dreams, you simply exist and die a little more each day. Take the time to dream big dreams and etch them into your mind with a clear picture of what your life will look like once you accomplish them.

Go for the Goals

The next step after dreaming big is to break those dreams down into individual S.M.A.R.T. goals to help you achieve those dreams.

S.M.A.R.T. stands for Specific, Measurable, Attainable, Relevant, and Time Bound.

S is for Specific. Make your goal as specific as possible. With clarity comes focus. You will be able to focus much better when your goal is as specific and clear as possible.

M is for Measurable. Add a unit of measure to your goal. You want to make X number of dollars, meet a potential soul mate with certain qualities, or start a business that specializes in one particular area.

A is for Attainable. Make sure your goal is realistic. If you have no business experience and want to be making

$1,000,000 at the end of your first year, that is clearly not realistic. If you have fifty or a hundred pounds to lose, and you would like to lose all that weight by next week, again, that is not going to happen. Set attainable goals and set yourself up for success, not failure.

R is for Relevant. Make sure your goal will bring you closer to accomplishing the big dream you are setting out to achieve.

T is for Time Bound. You need to set a deadline or it will never happen.

Don't Settle for Less

You can achieve anything you want with enough effort. Sometimes it takes longer to accomplish goals and dreams that are on the larger side. Just remember, all good things are worth waiting for. You just need to be sure you are moving toward your goal everyday.

O - Overcome Limiting Beliefs

"You can have anything you want if you will give up the belief that you can't have it."

~ Dr. Robert Anthony

Earl Nightingale said it best, "You become what you think about." It was once said that human beings have an average of 65,000 thoughts per day. Each one of these thoughts is either positively charged or negatively charged. There is no middle ground. Of these 65,000 thoughts, about 85 percent are negative for most people. This is precisely the reason you should step up and be more than most people.

You can do it. You just have to want to do it.

Avoid Self-Defeating Self-Talk

How often do you beat yourself up? If you make a mistake or something doesn't turn out the way you planned, do you riddle yourself with negative self-talk? Do you generalize and say things to yourself like, "I have a horrible sense of direction, or I'm terrible at remembering names, or I just can't seem to make ends meet?"

Every time you have one of these conversations with yourself, you are doing yourself a tremendous disservice. You are cheating yourself out of the chance of improving. The more you think poorly of yourself, the poorer you will become.

"Whether You Believe You Can or You Can't, You're Right!" ~ Henry Ford

It's often difficult to fathom the power of the mind. Your mind can be your best friend in the world or a sworn enemy. The choice is yours. How will you use your mind going forward?

I mentioned the next two points briefly in the beginning of the book, but they bear repeating.

Affirm With Affirmations

They don't need to be mushy and gushy, just positive. "The more grateful I am, the more reasons I find to be grateful," "I choose to make positive healthy choices for myself," "When I believe in myself, so do others," and my favorite from Michael Anthony's book, *How to be Happy and Have Fun Changing the World*, "I am always truthful, positive, and helping others." Imagine if everyone on the planet lived by those eight simple words how much better off the world would be.

Visualize What's Possible

Visualization is a powerful tool for creating your desired reality so that it can later manifest for you. Create a vision board, and keep it somewhere you will see it several times a day.

Do this by going through magazines and newspapers and clipping out images and words that give you joy and that you want to experience in your life. It creates a perfect reminder of what you are striving for and helps you stay focused on your goals.

C - Cultivate Relationships with Like-Minded People

"A true friend is one who knows all about you and likes you anyway."

~ Christi Mary Warner

Now, more than ever, it is easy to reach out and befriend people who think like you do.

Leverage Social Networking

It has been proven that your social network of friends can improve your happiness, and you can do the same for them.

With all the available networking tools today, there is no reason to sit in a dark corner and be alone. It's simple enough to go online, or even offline, to find people who have similar interests and interact with them.

Identify the Cheerleaders in Your Life

Once you begin hanging with people of like minds, you will find that you have many cheerleaders; people who truly want you to succeed and be happy. These are the folks you want to stay around.

It can be incredibly beneficial when you surround yourself with people who care about you, root for you, and cheer you on when you need it the most.

Eliminate the Dead Weight

Unfortunately, there is also the other side of the coin. There are people among us who are the picture of negativity. They can't seem to see the good in anything or anyone. It is best to stay far away from these people because they will only try to dampen your spirit and keep you from achieving your dreams.

It may be painful to let these people go if they play an important part in your life. Whether it is a parent, spouse, sibling, child, or close friend, if the culprit is holding you back and stealing your dreams, you may be well served to reduce or eliminate communication with them.

K - **Killer Quotes to Live By**

"Sometimes a great quote is all you need to make a point. See?"

~ Ricky Powell, the Happiness Guy

I have collected countless quotes on happiness over the years. Here are some of my favorites:

"Happiness is not an accident, nor is it something you wish for. Happiness is something you design." ~ Jim Rohn

"It is not the place, nor the condition, but the mind alone that can make anyone happy or miserable." ~ Roger L'Estrange

"The best way to find yourself is to lose yourself in the service of others." ~ Gandhi

"I think happiness is what makes you pretty. Happy people are beautiful." ~ Drew Barrymore

"Action may not always bring happiness; but there is no happiness without action." ~ Benjamin Disraeli

"Time you enjoy wasting was not wasted." ~ John Lennon

"Anyone who says sunshine brings happiness has never danced in the rain." ~ Unknown

"People are just about as happy as they make up their minds to be." ~ Abraham Lincoln

"For every minute you are angry you lose sixty seconds of happiness." ~ Ralph Waldo Emerson

"How little a thing can make us happy when we feel that we have earned it." ~ Mark Twain

"The secret of happiness is to make others believe that they are the cause of it." ~ Al Batt

"Happiness is a choice that requires effort at times." ~ Unknown

"Three grand essentials to happiness in this life are something to do, something to love, and something to hope for." ~ Joseph Addison

"True happiness is to enjoy the present, without anxious dependence upon the future." ~ Lucius Annaeus Seneca

"Success is not the key to happiness. Happiness is the key to success. If you love what you are doing, you will be successful." ~ Herman Cain

"There are hundreds of languages in the world, but a smile speaks them all." ~ Unknown

"Success is getting and achieving what you want. Happiness is wanting and being content with what you get." ~ Bernard Meltzer

"People will forget what you said, people will forget what you did, but people will never forget how you made them feel." ~ Maya Angelou

"The Constitution only guarantees the American people the right to pursue happiness. You have to catch it yourself." ~ Benjamin Franklin

"It is not how much we have, but how much we enjoy, that makes happiness." ~ Charles Haddon Spurgeon

"Some cause happiness wherever they go; others whenever they go." ~ Oscar Wilde

"Happiness is nothing more than good health and a bad memory." ~ Albert Schweitzer

"Happiness depends upon ourselves." ~ Aristotle

"If there were in the world today any large number of people who desired their own happiness more than they desired the unhappiness of others, we could have paradise in a few years." ~ Bertrand Russell

"Cherish all your happy moments: they make a fine cushion for old age." ~ Christopher Morley

"Sometimes it's hard to avoid the happiness of others." ~ David Assael

"The foolish man seeks happiness in the distance, the wise grows it under his feet." ~ James Oppenheim

"It is pretty hard to tell what does bring happiness; poverty and wealth have both failed." ~ Kin Hubbard

"Happiness is when what you think, what you say, and what you do are in harmony." ~ Mahatma Gandhi

"Very little is needed to make a happy life." ~ Marcus Aurelius Antoninus

"There is no cosmetic for beauty like happiness." ~ Countess of Blessington

"Happiness is a conscious choice, not an automatic response." ~ Mildred Barthel

"We all want to be happy, and we're all going to die. You might say those are the only two unchallengeably true facts that apply to every human being on this planet." ~ William Boyd

"Simply put, you believe that things or people make you unhappy, but this is not accurate. You make yourself unhappy." ~ Wayne Dyer

"Success is getting what you want, happiness is wanting what you get." ~ Dave Gardner

"The happiest people seem to be those who have no particular reason for being so except that they are so." ~ William Ralph Inge

"It is neither wealth nor splendor, but tranquility and occupation, which give happiness." ~ Thomas Jefferson

"We always have enough to be happy if we are enjoying what we do have—and not worrying about what we don't have." ~ Ken Keyes, Jr.

"The purpose of life is the expansion of happiness." ~ Maharishi Mahesh Yogi

"Happiness doesn't come from doing what we like to do but from liking what we have to do." ~ Wilfred A. Peterson

"Happiness is an attitude. We either make ourselves miserable or happy and strong. The amount of work is the same." ~ Francesca Reigler

"Most people ask for happiness on condition. Happiness can only be felt if you don't set any condition." ~ Arthur Rubinstein

"The good life, as I conceive it, is a happy life. I do not mean that if you are good you will be happy; I mean that if you are happy you will be good." ~ Bertrand Russell

"My life has no purpose, no direction, no aim, no meaning, and yet I'm happy. I can't figure it out. What am I doing right?" ~ Charles M. Schulz

"If you want to be happy, be." ~ Leo Tolstoy

"Human happiness and moral duty are inseparably connected." ~ George Washington

"Often people attempt to live their lives backwards; they try to have more things, or more money, in order to do more of what they want, so they will be happier." ~ Margaret Young

"The secret of contentment is knowing how to enjoy what you have and to be able to lose all desire for things beyond your reach." ~ Lin Yutang

"Whoever is happy will make others happy, too." ~ Mark Twain

"Happiness is a butterfly, which, when pursued, is always just beyond your grasp, but which, if you will sit down quietly, may alight upon you." ~ Nathaniel Hawthorne

"Life is to be fortified by many friendships. To love and to be loved is the greatest happiness of existence." ~ Sydney Smith

"Happiness is inward, and not outward; and so, it does not depend on what we have, but on what we are." ~ Henry Van Dyke

"The happiness of the bee and the dolphin is to exist. For man it is to know that and to wonder at it." ~ Jacques-Yves Cousteau

"This very moment is a seed from which the flowers of tomorrow's happiness grow." ~ Margaret Lindsey

"Happiness always looks small while you hold it in your hands, but let it go, and you learn at once how big and precious it is." ~ Maxim Gorky

"I am more and more convinced that our happiness or our unhappiness depends far more on the way we meet the events of life than on the nature of those events themselves." ~ Wilhelm von Humboldt

"Real happiness is cheap enough, yet how dearly we pay for its counterfeit." ~ Hosea Ballou

"The secret of happiness is to admire without desiring." ~ Carl Sandburg

"Whoever said money can't buy happiness didn't know where to shop." ~ Gertrude Stein

"Love is the condition in which the happiness of another person is essential to your own." ~ Robert Heinlein

"Your living is determined not so much by what life brings to you as by the attitude you bring to life; not so much by what happens to you as by the way your mind looks at what happens." ~ Kahlil Gibran

"I finally realized ... I am so happy that I am jealous of myself!" ~ Unknown

Notice the Common Theme

You can learn a lot from a good quote. Hopefully, you learned something from the quotes included above. They contain an obvious common theme throughout.

What I have gleaned from these words of wisdom is that happiness is indeed a choice to be made. Numerous studies have shown that after basic living standards have been met; more money does not necessarily cause greater happiness.

Happiness is a feeling, an attitude that comes from within. It is based on many internal human factors, which we all possess. It's up to each of us to learn what is involved in the development of our own happiness and then let happiness ensue once we understand it all.

It is my goal through writing, speaking, facilitating, and coaching on the subject of happiness to get you on the path to higher consciousness, greater happiness, and increased success in every area of your life.

S- Sharpen The Saw

Stephen Covey's seventh habit from his book,
The 7 Habits of Highly Successful People

There's an old tale about two woodcutters who are in the forest one day. Each has an ax of identical size and sharpness. Each woodcutter is standing before a tree identical in size to the other.

They are going to race to see who can cut down his tree the fastest. On the count of three, each woodcutter goes to work, feverishly cutting into his tree.

One wood cutter keeps cutting and cutting, while the other one stops every few minutes, walks a few paces away behind some bushes, then comes back and gets going again.

After almost an hour, the woodcutter who kept walking away had his tree cut down. The other woodcutter still had quite a bit of tree to cut through. He accused the first woodcutter of cheating. "How can you have cut all the way through your tree when you stopped and rested every few minutes while I have been cutting the whole time and still have not cut down my tree?"

The first wood cutter smiled and said, "I was not resting, my friend. Every time I noticed my saw getting dull from cutting, I stopped to sharpen my blade."

Sharpening the saw was important enough for Covey to write about, and you should take this advice to heart.

What exactly does sharpening your saw mean? Here are some suggestions:

* Exercise at least three to four times per week
* Improve your diet
* Educate yourself (read, listen to audio programs, attend a seminar)
* Learn a new skill or language

* Join a club or association
* Meditate
* Begin a journal
* Have a meaningful conversation with a friend or family member
* Set new goals or review/update your old goals
* Organize your home or office
* Go on a date
* Clear some tasks you've been putting off
* Read *Happiness Rocks*!

Become a Lifelong Learner

Most people think that once they are out of school, they are done being a student. In reality, it is important to always be a student of life. We are constantly either moving ahead or falling behind. There is no such thing as standing still. Why not improve yourself everyday by learning something new each day that can help you thrive in life? For the most part, it's what you learn after school that is the most helpful and important.

Always Be Creating

Never rest on your laurels. Carry a notepad or a digital recorder with you at all times. Ideas come when you least expect them. You could be in bed, in the shower, in the car, anywhere at all. The bad news is, ideas evaporate as quickly as they materialize. If you don't capture them immediately you can kiss them good-bye. We lose too many brilliant thoughts this way. Always be creating, and always be capturing. Then, it's time to act!

Pass It On

Once you begin to gain the wisdom you seek, you are only halfway there. You must pass along your newfound brilliance to the world. Share your knowledge with others. When you read or hear a meaningful quote, don't keep it to yourself. Pass it onto your friends and loved ones. When you hear an idea worth repeating, repeat it. It's all too easy to keep quiet. Be better than that. Be strong, be true, and make a difference. Don't just leave this earth one day: leave a legacy.

PART THREE

Final Thoughts

Masterminds of Lifelong Happiness

You have no doubt heard the expression, "Two heads are better than one." Imagine how much better six or eight or ten heads would be.

Masterminds have been around through the ages. From King Arthur and the Knights of the Round Table, to the Founding Fathers of the United States, to some of the most successful business minds and thought leaders in history—from Alexander Graham Bell and Thomas A. Edison to Henry Ford. When great minds come together anything is possible.

Here's the concept:

I can write or speak all day long on the subject of happiness. You may be able to read or listen all day as well. However, unless we all practice what we learn everyday, it just doesn't stick.

There are many benefits that come with belonging to a supportive mastermind group:

You have a number of people available to help you succeed.

You receive the benefit of varied perspectives, input, and feedback.

You have the opportunity to gain resources and connections through your group that you may not have otherwise had on your own.

You receive inspiration and accountability from the group, which helps you focus on achieving your goals.

Introducing Masterminds of Lifelong Happiness. Soon, we'll be offering virtual and live mastermind groups where you will receive all these benefits and so much more.

In addition to these mastermind groups, there will be opportunities to attend live retreats as well as individual mentoring programs for those who qualify.

For more information on our Masterminds of Lifelong Happiness groups and live events or to apply for our individual mentoring programs, please visit, www. LifelongHappiness.com.

Your New Beginning

"The secret to a rich life is to have more beginnings than endings."

~ David Weinbaum

It's time to discuss the elephant in the room. On each of the preceding pages, I have done my best to inspire you to rethink what's possible. However, the reality is that no one can make you happy but you.

You can read this book and many others like it, but ultimately, you need to ask yourself the $64,000 question: "Am I ready to master the art of Lifelong Happiness by practicing the powerful blueprint I have just read?" I truly hope your answer is a resounding, "Yes!"

Regardless of whether or not you are ready to commit to the blueprint at this moment, I want you to know that I am here for you. I would be honored and grateful to be your happiness champion. If you'll allow me the privilege, I will do everything possible to help keep you on the journey to enlightenment.

I can be your accountability partner, mentor, and trusted advisor who can help you attain the wondrous riches that await you out there in the vast unknown. Will you let me help you? If so, I can promise you this: I will never give up on you. What I will need from you, though, is your commitment that you will never give up on yourself.

As I hope you've learned by now, the only way to fail in life is to simply give up. As long as you keep trying and moving forward, you cannot fail. There will be times when you stumble and make mistakes. These setbacks are part of what makes you human.

Remember, it's how you respond to these setbacks that truly sets you apart from the masses. Most people get discouraged and give up long before giving themselves a chance to succeed.

Deep inside, I always knew that one day I would become an author and write a book on a subject I was passionate about. It was just a matter of setting a goal, taking small measureable steps each day, and not letting anything stand in the way of that goal.

If you would like to live a life filled with passion, happiness, and success, I highly recommend you decide what subject you love most, then go to work on creating a hobby or business centered on that topic. There are so many ways to create a space online that can provide you the opportunity to achieve great results, whether financial or simply gaining notoriety in your chosen area of interest.

Taking on a hobby, or a part-time or full-time business that is focused on something you love, can be life changing. It certainly has been for me.

I'm about to begin work on my second book, which will specifically address this topic and help you find that passion and decide the best way to go about turning it into a tangible asset, which can provide a lifetime of happiness and even financial rewards if that is what you are seeking.

Action Steps for Today

Please visit LifelongHappiness.com right now. Take a moment to sign up to receive my free e-course, *How to Overcome the 7 Toxic Beliefs About Happiness Which Keep You From Being Happy*. Not only will you receive invaluable information about these seven devastating beliefs and how to avoid them, you will also receive the opportunity to stay in touch with me so that I can notify you of upcoming events, products, or services I feel may benefit you in the future.

Next, go to TheHappinessGuy.com to register for your free *TGIT Daily Dose of Inspiration* e-mail. We're all familiar with, "Working for the Weekend" and thinking, "Thank God It's Friday!" TGIT turns that thought around to, "Thank God It's Today!" There is no reason you can't wake up every morning, jump out of bed, and be grateful to be alive, ready to start a new day. This short, daily dose of inspiration will help you do just that.

Please also visit HappinessRocksSystem.com for the entire *Happiness Rocks Home Study Course* if you haven't already done so. It is my belief that making this investment in yourself is the single most important action you can take to further your knowledge of the subject as well as your chances of making this commitment to happiness a daily practice. I've done it; you can, too.

Notice I wrote, "Practice" and not, "Pursuit." That's because we don't want to pursue happiness, we want to work with the tools outlined in this book so that happiness can ensue naturally from how we are living with our reinvented selves.

Now, my friend, it's up to you. Your journey begins here. I challenge you to make each day of the rest of your life a positive, powerful force that will propel you to whatever level of success you desire in every area of your life.

Thank You and God Bless,

Ricky Powell,
The Happiness Guy